THE DUNG BEETLE SEARCH AND FIND GUIDE

I SAW AN ART FAIR

*Written and illustrated by
Miriam Elia*

© 2025

Art Fair Sponsored by a dubious Middle Eastern theocracy.

Have you ever been to an art fair? Can you even afford to get into an art fair? Whether you sneak in for free or steal a Russian Oligarch's bankcard, Dung Beetle books proudly presents a handy and simple 'spotting' guide.

There is so much to see that appears original at the art fair, and yet the thought awakens that you might have seen most of it before.

From mannequins in shopping trolleys to skulls with flashy things in them, as you spot artworks in a similar style you earn an I-SAW score for yourself.
You'll find your score will quickly mount up, and when it totals 1,250 points you may award yourself the rank of CULTURALLY AWAKENED.

ABOUT DUNG BEETLE

Dung Beetle Books Ltd was founded in 2015 by Miriam Elia, an artist who is deeply committed to not being inclusive, diverse or sustainable.

I-SAW An Art Fair

A giant sculpture of a cartoon character *with a psychotic thousand-yard stare.*

I-SAW on (date) ....

at..and

scored   **40**   points ◯

I-SAW An Art Fair

Cartoon meltdown
evoking rapid or disastrous decline and collapse.

I-SAW on (date) ....

at..and

scored   **30**   points ◯

I-SAW An Art Fair

Melodramatic depiction of the imminent climate catastrophe.

I-SAW on (date) ....

at...and

scored **40** points ○

I-SAW An Art Fair

A **stack of TV sets** on the floor displaying a view of the sea on a bad day.

I-SAW on (date) ....

at..and

scored   **40**   points ◯

I-SAW An Art Fair

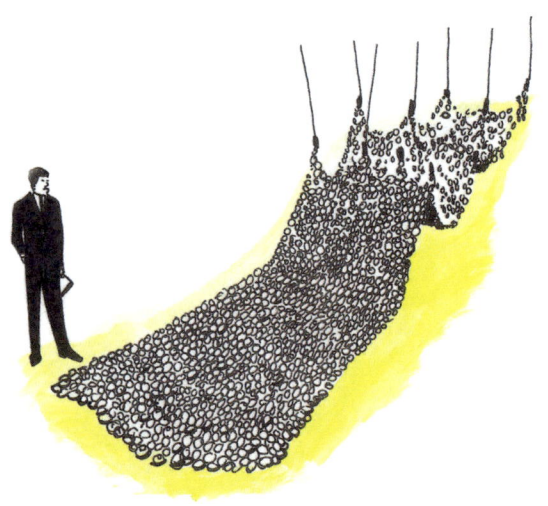

Fussy bits and bobs, strung up into heavy chains of oppression.

I-SAW on (date) ....

at..and

scored **30** points ◯

I-SAW An Art Fair

A craftless piece of craft.
Torn-up fabric hanging from the ceiling.

I-SAW on (date) ....

at..and

scored **20** points ◯

I-SAW An Art Fair

A big trashy skull.
Money and materialism are meaningless, except if you don't have any money.

I-SAW on (date) ....

at..and

scored **30** points ◯

A big flashy diamond-covered skull.
We are all equal in death but some people have a lot more money in life.

I-SAW on (date) ....

at..and

scored **30** points ○

I-SAW An Art Fair

Squiggly Blobby child-like things blobbing around.

I-SAW on (date) ....

at..and

scored **15** points ○

I-SAW An Art Fair

A sculpture that resembles the **unravelling of the lower intestines.**

I-SAW on (date) ....

at..and

scored   **25**   points ◯

I-SAW An Art Fair

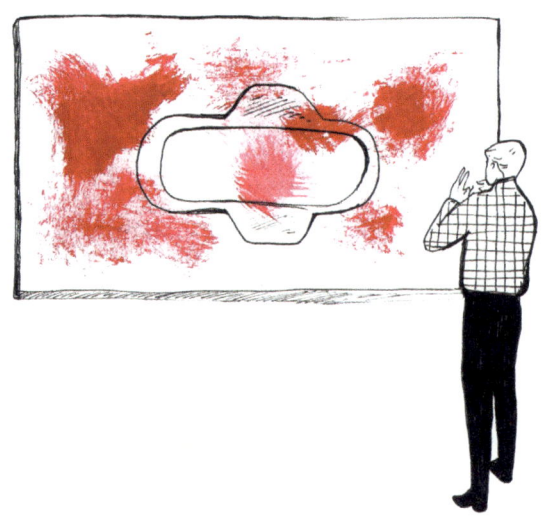

Expressive Sanitary Towel.
Like an unfertilised egg, we are all about to die.

I-SAW on (date) ....

at..and

scored   **50**   points ◯

I-SAW An Art Fair

Assemblage of broken dolls and crucifixes.
Arranged like votive offerings.

I-SAW on (date) ....

at..and

scored **15** points ◯

I-SAW An Art Fair

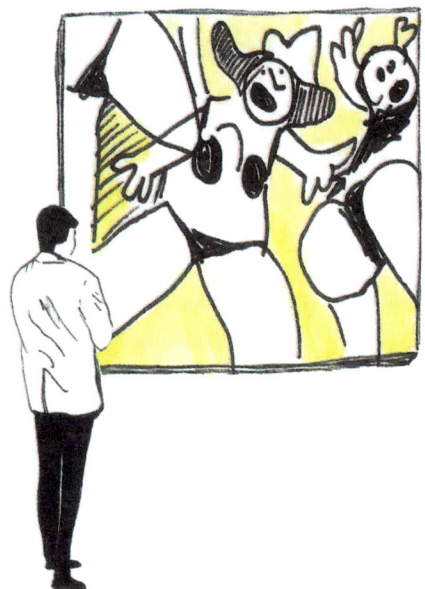

Huge **Porno-Naive** painting of strippers being brazen.

I-SAW on (date) ....

at..and

scored   **40**   points ◯

I-SAW An Art Fair

Dribbly Botox Lips in different shades of dribble.

I-SAW on (date) ....

at...and

scored   **25**   points ◯

I-SAW An Art Fair

Not collapsing, collapsing sculpture.

I-SAW on (date) ....

at..and

scored **50** points ○

I-SAW An Art Fair

An **upside down church**.
That nobody is able to turn the right way up.

I-SAW on (date) ....

at..and

scored **20** points ◯

I-SAW An Art Fair

Chaotic **pile of chairs** that you can't sit on because they are post-modern.

I-SAW on (date) ....

at..and

scored   **5**   points ◯

I-SAW An Art Fair

Worthless tables that have collapsed even further into post-post modernism.

I-SAW on (date) ....

at..and

scored   **0**   points ◯

I-SAW An Art Fair

A soft play **Rainbow Sculpture.**

I-SAW on (date) ....

at..and

scored **45** points ◯

I-SAW An Art Fair

A shocking stencil image that isn't shocking.

I-SAW on (date) ....

at...and

scored   **20**   points ◯

I-SAW An Art Fair

Stone-Age figures, floating about and killing each other.

I-SAW on (date) ....

at..and

scored **25** points ◯

I-SAW An Art Fair

A **Wokem Pole**.
A mushed up pile of oppressed global victims.

I-SAW on (date) ....

at..and

scored **5** points ◯

I-SAW An Art Fair

Post-Apocalyptic tentacles of regrowth
After the human race has hopefully died out.

I-SAW on (date) ....

at...and

scored   **20**   points ○

I-SAW An Art Fair

Giant fruit or vegetable sculpture
Plant-based worship for misanthropic outlook.

I-SAW on (date) ....

at...and

scored **5** points ○

I-SAW An Art Fair

A **self-harming artist** flirts with pain and death by pretending to suffocate in a plastic bag.

I-SAW on (date) ....

at..and

scored   **50**   points ◯

I-SAW An Art Fair

A pseudo-subversive stencil *convincing you that the terrorist is actually a really nice chap.*

I-SAW on (date) ....

at...and

scored **25** points ◯

b) A long, boring train journey.

d) A miserable old person mumbling.

and scored points   **20**   points

I-SAW An Art Fair

Huge smug beer can penis.

I-SAW on (date) ....

at..and

scored **30** points ○

I-SAW An Art Fair

Crap Picasso homage.

I-SAW on (date) ....

at..and

scored   **10**   points ◯

I-SAW An Art Fair

Squiggly Inner Turmoil Journey.

I-SAW on (date) ....

at..and

scored **2** points ○

I-SAW An Art Fair

A **miserable grey wash** painting to cheer you up on a rainy day.

I-SAW on (date) ....

at..and

scored **4** points ○

I-SAW An Art Fair

Conceptual artist trying to paint.

I-SAW on (date) ....

at..and

scored **100 million** points

I-SAW An Art Fair

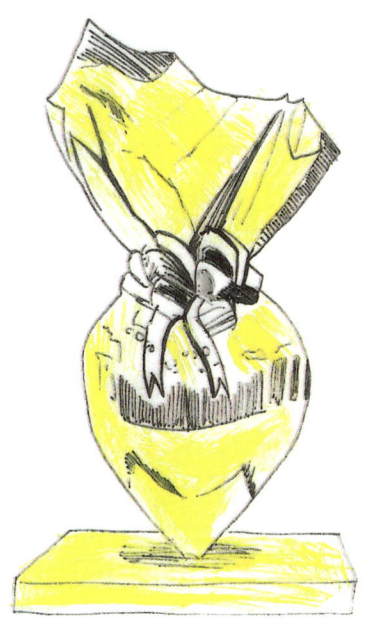

Vacuous vacuum-packed object.

I-SAW on (date) ....

at..and

scored   **10**   points ○

I-SAW An Art Fair

AI generated immersive wank.

I-SAW on (date) ....

at..and

scored **2** points ◯

I-SAW An Art Fair

Neon Platitudes.
In the style of Clinton's Cards.

I-SAW on (date) ....

at..and

scored **15** points ◯

I-SAW An Art Fair

Dismembered mannequins in a shopping trolley.

I-SAW on (date) ....

at..and

scored **10** points ◯

I-SAW An Art Fair

Dismembered mannequin scattered around a shopping trolley.

I-SAW on (date) ....

at...and

scored **10** points ○

I-SAW An Art Fair

Humans playing animals playing humans.

I-SAW on (date) ....

at..and

scored **2** points ◯

I-SAW An Art Fair

Fabulous after-party you are not invited to.

I-SAW on (date) ....

at...and

scored **1000** points ◯

Other Dung Beetle Titles

The Diary of Edward the Hamster (1990-1990)	2012
We go to the gallery	2014
We learn at home	2016
We go out	2016
Isis in Sylvania	2017
We do Christmas	2018
Piggy goes to University	2018
We do Lockdown	2020
We see the sights	2022
Marina & the curse of the Royal Yugoslavian Academy of Art	2023
Things to make and do	2023

Notes / Things I found offensive

Book Design Becky Philp Published by Miriam Elia, Dung Beetle Books Ltd, London
ISBN 978-1-7391442-3-4 © DUNG BEETLE BOOKS LTD 2025

Order of Merit
awarded to

_____

of

_____

_____
FULL NAME AND ADDRESS HERE

I-Saw spotter no_____ in the I-Saw-Tribe earning the Honourable Rank of Culturally Awakened and Completely Brainwashed

Witnessed by | (Adult) for Big Artist Miriam I-Saw

First Class Honours
1250 points
awarded on

Stamp Here